Van Gogh *by* Van Eck

A Musical Journey Into The Heart and Soul of Vincent van Gogh

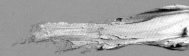

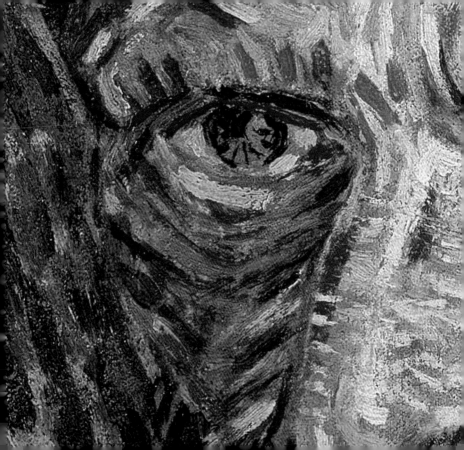

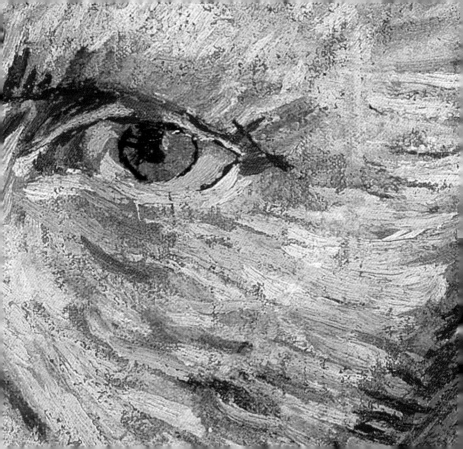

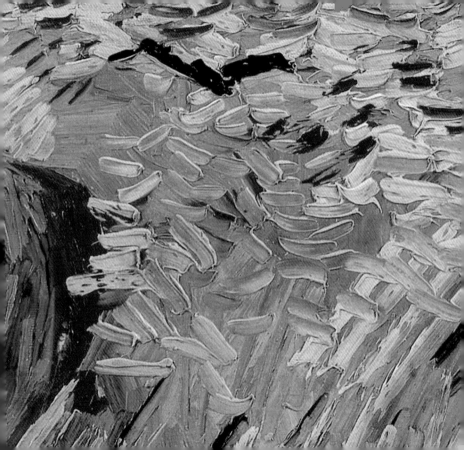

"I cannot help it that my pictures do not sell.
Nevertheless the time will come when people will see
that they are worth more than the price of the paint..."

VINCENT VAN GOGH was an artist of the senses like no other. A viewer is struck with the immediacy of passion and angst transmitted by his startling interplay of color and texture. The vibrant, tumultuous images that characterize his swirling brushstrokes bridge 130 years, sweeping us into the moment of his spontaneous creation as if then were now. Vincent painted as he lived: with ardor, insight, pathos, fervor, vibrancy and love. He furiously scribbled letters to his brother Theo day after day, leaving behind an articulate and vivid paper trail of images and insights.

They're all there for us to read: the soaring dreams, the illusions held and shattered. We feel the sting of the cruel blows that were dealt him by the sheer inequities that challenged his life. Each of us rejoices and cries with Vincent van Gogh with the vehemence of a lover. Through these paintings and letters documenting his every mood, his love affair with color, the tortures of his heart and the brilliance of his art, we each embark on a journey into his very soul, jolted by lightening-bolts of insight as to what drove him to the creative heights and plunged him to the depths of self-destruction.

It is this compelling visual stimulus that sparked an idea. Dutch recording artist Van Eck pondered how the inspiration of his fellow countryman could be channeled into other of the senses through the medium of Music. He embarked on a journey to interpret the artist's work through song. As the project began to take shape, he was brought together with Pamela Phillips Oland and Tom Harriman, two accomplished songwriters in Los Angeles. Van Eck expressed his desire to honor Vincent's art in music, and the two responded with a musical life-story narrated as if through the voice of Vincent himself, inspired by his own paintings that spoke of pivotal moments in his artistic and personal life. With impassioned arrangements and production by Tom Harriman, the year-long process of writing and recording Van Gogh by Van Eck included the talents of several of the world's most gifted musicians, and recordings at the fabled Capitol Records Studios in Hollywood, California. Finally, Grammy®-winning designer Andy Engel wove together the sensations of sound and color in a unique packaging that sweeps us up into this Musical Journey into the Heart and Soul of **VINCENT VAN GOGH.**

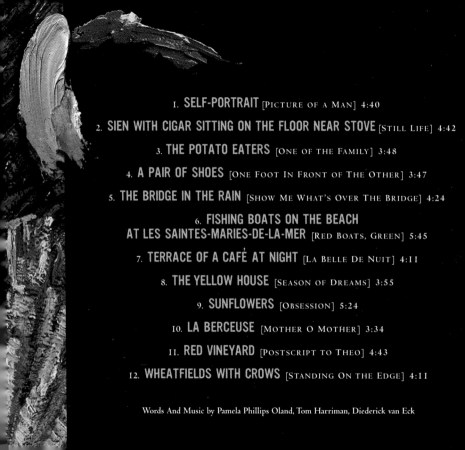

1. SELF-PORTRAIT [Picture of a Man] 4:40

2. SIEN WITH CIGAR SITTING ON THE FLOOR NEAR STOVE [Still Life] 4:42

3. THE POTATO EATERS [One of the Family] 3:48

4. A PAIR OF SHOES [One Foot In Front of The Other] 3:47

5. THE BRIDGE IN THE RAIN [Show Me What's Over The Bridge] 4:24

6. FISHING BOATS ON THE BEACH
AT LES SAINTES-MARIES-DE-LA-MER [Red Boats, Green] 5:45

7. TERRACE OF A CAFÉ AT NIGHT [La Belle De Nuit] 4:11

8. THE YELLOW HOUSE [Season of Dreams] 3:55

9. SUNFLOWERS [Obsession] 5:24

10. LA BERCEUSE [Mother O Mother] 3:34

11. RED VINEYARD [Postscript to Theo] 4:43

12. WHEATFIELDS WITH CROWS [Standing On the Edge] 4:11

Words And Music by Pamela Phillips Oland, Tom Harriman, Diederick van Eck

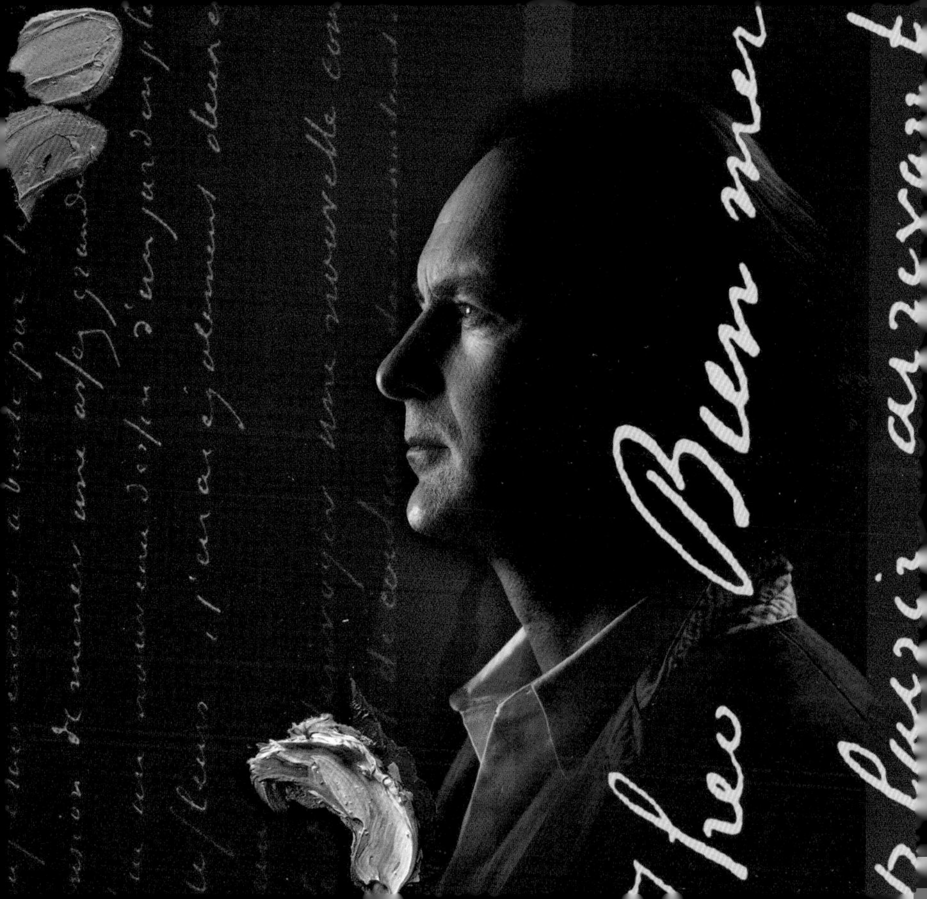

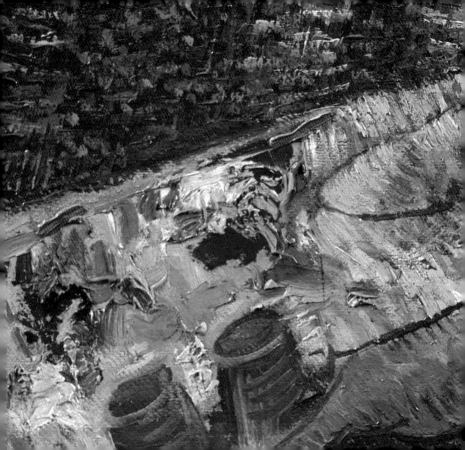

"They say—and I am very well to believe it—
that it is difficult to know yourself—
but it isn't easy to paint yourself either."

PORTRAIT OF THE ARTIST

There are over 30 of them in all, the self portraits In them we see: a face glittering eyed, hollow-eyed, blue-eyed, sad-eyed; a haunted face; a face distorted by self-loathing; the face of a man with a lifelong desire to be known and understood.

He paints himself, always unsmiling, ever bearded, head shaved like a Monk, sporting a straw boater, a fur cap, or a grey felt hat with a satin ribbon. Canvases from spring 1886 to September 1889 draw us into the many faces of Vincent, as he records his ever-volatile emotions and self-doubts, his sanity, and his descent into madness. And now we ask which is the real Vincent van Gogh

I may not be a fashionable man, or someone you find easy to understand. Forgive me if I don't share your views. If I refuse it's 'cause I'm only good at being who I am. Am I invisible – or do you just see through me? And do you see me clear through the shadows that pursue me? Will there come a day when you'll know me, get me, see me? Or ever understand what it's like – what it means – to be me? Am I the man in the picture, or the Picture of a Man? My colors speak the words I cannot find. They say it all between the lines. But maybe it's a portrait of lies, and changing eyes. You'll know the face I've already left behind. Am I invisible – or do you just see through me? And do you see me clear through the shadows that pursue me? Will there come a day when you'll know me, get me, see me? Or ever understand what it's like – what it means – to be me? Am I the man in the picture, or the Picture of a Man? On this shifting canvas, nothing stays the same. Life just keeps on moving like a dancing flame. People think they know me – all they know is my name. Will there come a day when you'll know me, get me, see me? Or ever understand what it's like – what it means – to be me? Am I the man in the picture...or the Picture of a Man?

[PICTURE OF A MAN]

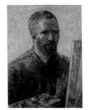

"SELF-PORTRAIT"
Arles, 188
van Gogh Museum, Amsterda

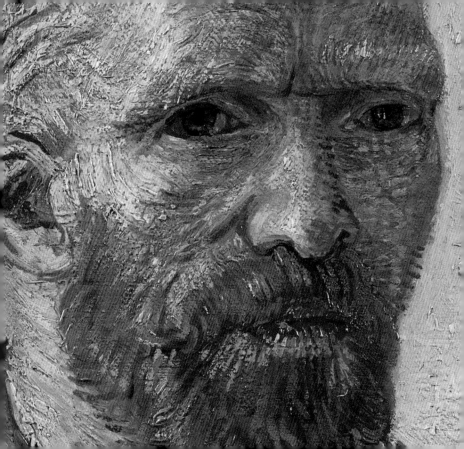

[STILL LIFE]

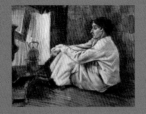

So this is who I need. Crazy how it turns out. Funny how it works out. Look what one girl can do. What a revelation, such an inspiration, when someone you love loves you. She is who I love. That's all I need to know. I was unprepared, that's true, but even so, here I am this time unafraid to fall. And the sweet simple wonder of it all is I belong. Everything has changed. Still life goes on. I've drawn her in my mind. Trying to invent her. Maybe heaven sent her to unlock the heart in me. What a revelation. No imagination came close to what love can be. I couldn't know how love can fill life. Love was a still life. Until life opened my eyes. She is who I love. That's all I need to know. I was unprepared, that's true, but even so, here I am this time unafraid to fall. And the sweet simple wonder of it all is I belong. Everything has changed. Still life goes on.

The more in tune we feel with Vincent, the more we long for him to have found happiness in a loving relationship. How is it a man with so much love and passion in his heart and soul could only long for that miracle to find him? And yet there was Sien, a woman who sold her body for money to support her child; Sien, who suddenly found herself adored and taken care of by a wild-eyed red-headed painter. For a while, Sien was his muse, his reason for being, his family, his someone to come home to. How he longed for Theo and the family to accept his choice without judgment.

SIEN
WITH CIGAR SITTING
ON THE
FLOOR NEAR STOVE

"SIEN WITH CIGAR SITTING ON
THE FLOOR NEAR STOVE"
The Hague, 188
Kröller-Müller Museum, Otter

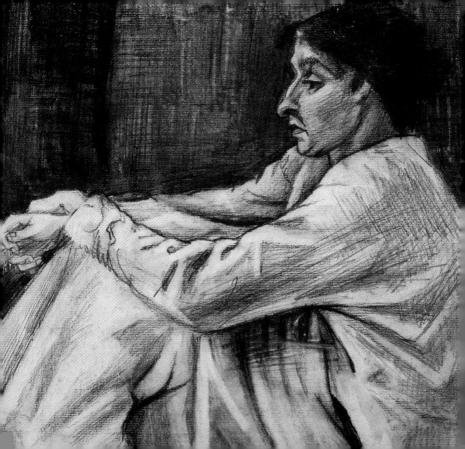

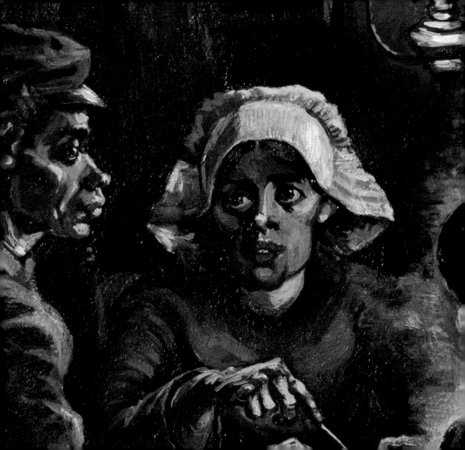

THE POTATO EATERS

[ONE OF THE FAMILY]

She sets the table for the family, and sets an extra place for company. The children call me and we gather round the light. I'm one of them tonight...one of the family tonight. He comes in cold and damp and glad he's home. I watch him share a joy that few have known. Someday I'll paint the shapes and colors of this sight, but I'm one of them tonight...one of the family tonight. Does he know – I see a lucky man, as only someone can like me, who's seen what life can be. They draw me in and ask about my day. I never thought I'd have so much to say. I see such beauty by the pale and naked light. I'm one of them tonight...one of the family tonight. I feel the tears to know that this will end. They've got each other, but I'm just a friend. So much to savor and relive some other night, but I'm one of them tonight...one of the family tonight.

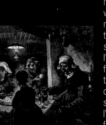

We sense his longing to belong to a family like this one, as he sits – a part, but apart – of the life in this spare, dark kitchen lit by a single bare flame. We smell the steam coming off the potatoes – just as he wanted us to; and the black tea will warm our chilled bodies in this farmer's hovel in Nuenen. Vincent notices, with quiet heartache, the way the wife's soft eyes seek her husband's approval and attention; his brush conjures the two women's hands, gnarled, old before their time; the child is still faceless, like his own longed-for children.

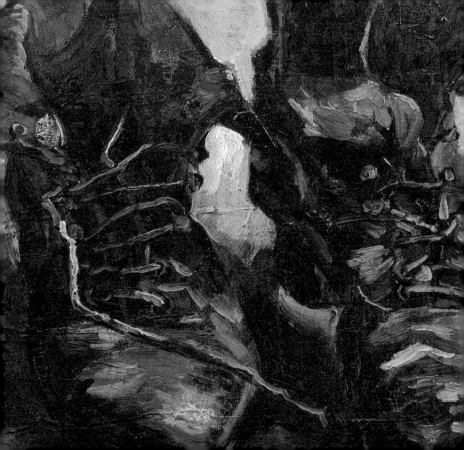

A PAIR
OF SHOES [ONE FOOT IN FRONT OF THE OTHER]

urning with disappointment over shattering romantic rejections by young Eugenie Loyer in ondon and his widowed cousin Kee in Etten, and the parting with Sien in the Hague; Vincent on the other hand encouraged by responses to his first masterwork, "The Potato Eaters." Ve visualize Vincent, excited at the thought of studying in Paris at the Atelier Cormon with oulouse-Lautrec and Emile Bernard. Yet he is an originator who is made to feel an outsider. o he paints every day, inventing his life as he goes along. He must keep moving forward oggedly, in spite of whatever holds him back, stands in his way, saddens or chagrins him.

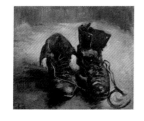

"A PAIR OF SHOES"
Paris, 1886
van Gogh Museum, Amsterdam

Trouble – creepin' 'round the corner. Trouble – bargin' through the door. Trouble – strikes without a warning. But when I'm out and down on the floor, I take a good hard look at the road, and I find there's only the one ahead and the one behind, and I put one foot in front of the other, cause I can't go back. One step'll lead to another, if I stay on track. If I wanna get where life is sweet, gotta start with my feet, and put one foot in front of the other, cause I can't go back. Money – slipping through my fingers. Women – shattering my heart. Worry – Where's it gonna get me? Just round an' round and I'm back at the start. Nobody else is walkin' the road in my shoes. No point in trippin' up on yesterday's news so I put one foot in front of the other, cause I can't go back. One step'll lead to another, if I stay on track. If I wanna get where life is sweet, gotta start with my feet, and put one foot in front of the other, cause I can't go back.

THE BRIDGE IN THE RAIN

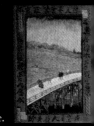

We shadow Vincent as he plunges headlong into a dazzling discovery of color, entranced by the flood of Japanoiserie that has taken Paris by storm. He has bought 200 prints of this Japanese art, studying the work of their masters, sometimes copying it in his own inimitable style, in all the vivid colors that have sparked his imagination. He reveres and is animated by all the artists who have come before him and whose art informs his work. Vincent paints a tribute to Hiroshige's "Ohashi Bridge in the Rain," yet what he produces is uniquely Vincent's own style and brush stroke. We hear Vincent's voice rising from his canvas, remarking that the answers to his thirst for the unknown surely await him on the other side of the bridge. He just has to make that crossing.

I am emerging like morning from night. A traveler on the bridge from darkness to light. The colors dazzle me with exotica and erotica. Heaven is where you find your muse. Hell is the street of dreams. You're chosen before you ever choose. Art is such a tease. Show Me What's Over The Bridge. Show me the side that I can't see. Show Me What's Over The Bridge. We see the same things differently. Enlighten me. I hold the brush but I don't paint alone; I'm here with every painter I've ever known. Take me beyond what I can visualize through these open eyes. Heaven is where you find your fire. Hell is the endless night. Compared to the colors you inspire, dreams are black and white.

[SHOW ME WHAT'S OVER THE BRIDGE]

"THE BRIDGE IN THE RAIN" [AFTER HIROSHIGE]
Paris, 18
van Gogh Museum, Amsterdam

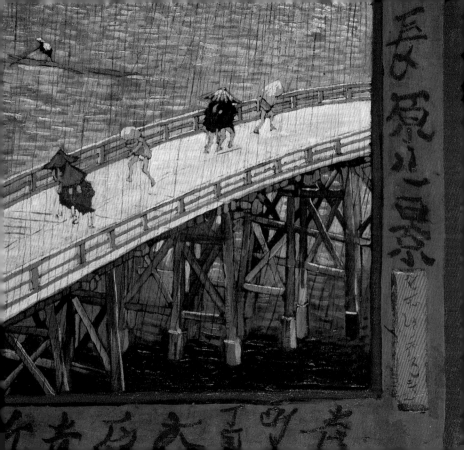

FISHING BOATS

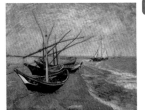

ON THE BEACH AT LES SAINTES-MARIES-DE-LA-MER

The smell of salty kelp wafts into our nostrils and stings our eyes. Sea breezes blow across our cheeks. We follow Vincent from Arles on a rare journey to the beach; he has traveled 36 kilometers to enjoy a couple of emotionally healing days in blessed solitude and pleasure communing with nature. The boats beached in repose not only present him with vivid color in stark relief against the white sands; but they also suggest images of where the sailors have been, and where they have yet to go.

White sails away on a mackerel sea. They catch the blush of the morning light. White gulls soar in a pink sky. I watch them fly till they're out of sight. Red Boats, green boats, yellow and grey. Fishermen netting their catch of the day. Brown boats, blue boats, orange and black. Gotta fill the hold before they turn back. My senses fill with salty seaweed. The world stops here on a gold sand dune, with hermit crabs in borrowed shells between the sun and the quarter moon. Red Boats, green boats, yellow and grey. Fishermen netting their catch of the

[RED BOATS, GREEN] day. Brown boats, blue boats, orange and black. Gotta fill the hold before they turn back. Sailboats are beached in a long bright line. They're leaning out yearning for the sea, like flowers reaching for the sun. Awaiting tides that will set them free. Red Boats, green boats, yellow and grey. Fishermen netting their catch of the day. Brown boats, blue boats, orange and black. Gotta fill the hold before they turn back.

"FISHING BOATS ON THE BEACH AT LES SAINTES-MARIES-DE-LA-MER"
Arles/Saintes-Maries, 1888
van Gogh Museum, Amsterdam

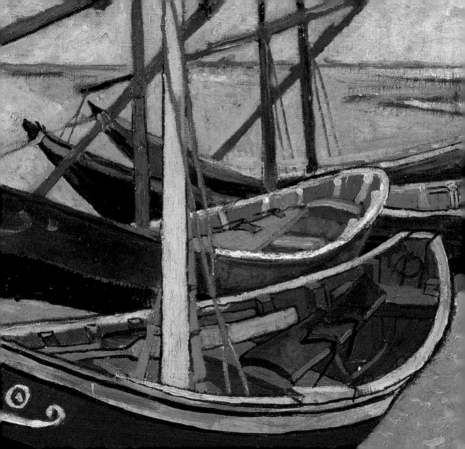

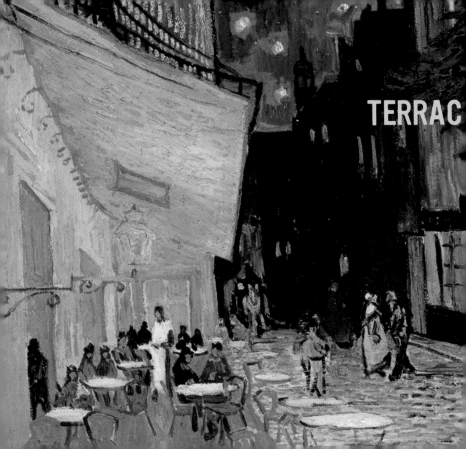
TERRAC

F A CAFÉ AT NIGHT

She is shadowed by the gaslight, a woman at once unreachable and completely desirable. She presides like a queen of some nocturnal world at her café table, aloof and somehow remote from the stares and chatter she invites. She is always alone, even when surrounded by followers and men seeking her favors. Vincent has a strange kinship with her vulnerabilities, wondering at her past. Her beauty draws him to her there on the terrace beneath his absurdly beautiful starry sky. Both are perhaps longing for some unrequited love; each of them caught in the web of yearned-for dreams, prey of the inky spider of night.

Maybe she'll be there tonight, beautiful and dangerous. La Belle de Nuit, at her favorite table. Eyes so full of promises in my darkest fantasies. Ma Belle de Nuit…will she look for me? La Belle de Nuit dreams of all the lovely things she meant to be. La Belle de Nuit. She'll face the life she never planned, a glass of courage in her hand. The future of her past is still a mystery. Just another falling star landing in a shadow world. La Belle de Nuit. Does she know she's beautiful? La Belle de Nuit dreams of all the lovely things she meant to be. La Belle de Nuit. She'll face the life she never planned, a glass of courage in her hand. The future of her past is still a mystery. Angel! Madonna of the rainy day. Heaven's just a prayer away. La Belle de Nuit. In her eyes the truth is plain, memories have left a stain like watercolors running in the rain. La Belle de Nuit…will she look for me. Beauty of the night. Do you know you're beautiful? La Belle de Nuit dreams of all the lovely things she meant to be. La Belle de Nuit. She'll face the life she never planned. A glass of courage in her hand. The future of her past is still a mystery. Beautiful and dangerous….

[LA BELLE DE NUIT]

"TERRACE OF A CAFÉ AT NIGHT"
Arles, 1888
Kröller-Müller Museum, Otterlo

THE YELLOW HOUSE [SEASON OF DREAMS]

Vincent nurtures a lifelong yearning to create an artists' colony — a place of communal life, a center for the exchange of ideas — where a brotherhood of artists can work, critique each other, and discuss the fine points of art. In 1888, he makes the move to Arles for the southern light. He rents the "Yellow House" on the Rue Lamartine, hoping fellow painters from Paris will follow. His brother and patron Theo van Gogh convinces the popular Paul Gauguin, a painter already of some standing, to move to the Yellow House and be the first to breathe life into Vincent's brotherhood. We feel Vincent's nervous energy in wanting to create a home-like atmosphere for Paul. He is clearly consumed with competing emotions: dread that the relationship will be a disaster, and hope that his Artist's Colony will finally come to life here at the house in the sun.

26

Alone — wrapped in the cloak of night, under a blaze of starry light. One seed — sown in a field of prayers was nurtured by toil and tears...all these years. I've found my place, now it seems this is the season of dreams. I've drawn the sketch — set the scene for the Yellow House on the Place Lamartine. Crossing the bridge of fools. Knowing that I don't know the rules. My hopes — carry me on their wings. Wanting the wishful things... this house brings. I've found my place, now it seems this is the season of dreams. I've drawn the sketch — set the scene for the Yellow House on the Place Lamartine. How do you make a house a home? What do you do? And can I ever match the picture that I drew? Now it's just beds and chairs, and secrets that wait beyond the stairs. A door leading to what might be. Leading to you and me... turn the key. I've found my place, now it seems this is the season of dreams. I've drawn the sketch — set the scene for the Yellow House, on the Place Lamartine.

"THE YELLOW HOUSE
Arles, 1888
van Gogh Museum, Amsterdam

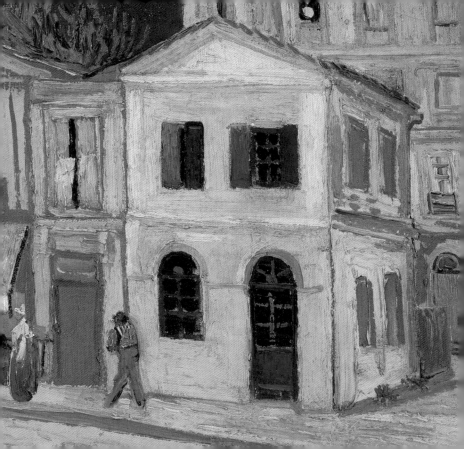

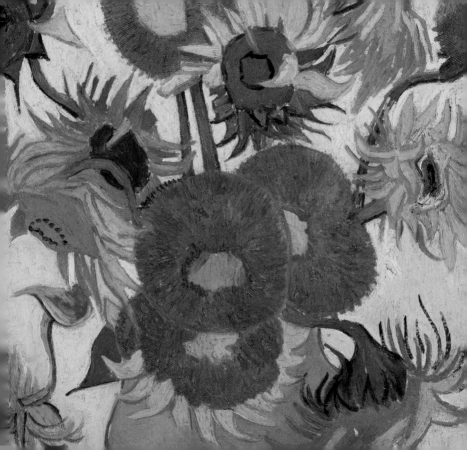

Traces of yellow cadmium paint smudged his white smock, as Vincent eagerly hung a myriad of glorious sunflower canvases across the walls of the room Paul Gauguin was to occupy. He was obsessed with the hope that now, finally, his dream of creating an artist's colony would be realized. But in the two months since Paul arrived, they have had a tempestuous, stormy relationship interspersed with uneasy truces. They have painted side-by-side in the fields and valleys of Arles' lush sun-drenched countryside, two painters enjoying the perfect light for their art. But in Paul's view, Vincent has become crushingly needy, and now Paul is staying away from the Yellow House, sometimes all night. Vincent sees everything crumbling, and follows him one night. Paul - who is perhaps just a bit jealous of Vincent's genius—turns and snarls at him to get lost. Vincent rushes home, and in a punishing fury of hurt and frustration, cuts off the lobe and tragus of his left ear with a straight razor.

SUNFLOWERS

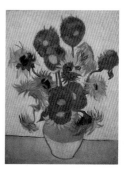

Tiny little cuts. Nothing you would notice. Tiny little pieces of my soul escaping. Wicked little cuts, sparing no emotion. Hear my muses laughing at the dream they stole. Can he feel the heat, hopes that burn inside me? And can he feed the hungers of my heart that drive me? Both of us complete, when he paints beside me. Close as sun on water in our worlds apart. Obsession! A tempest whirling around and round. This passion, a vision lost and so nearly found. Obsession! But does he share it at all? Flaring gold as the sunflowers that I painted – to hang on Gauguin's wall. Tiny little cuts, slashing at my reason. Whittling away at every lofty notion. Painful little nicks, learning he believes in living for the moment and not the love. Obsession! A tempest whirling around and round. This passion, a vision lost and so nearly found. Obsession! But does he share it at all? Flaring gold as the sunflowers that I painted – to hang on Gauguin's wall. What's one more cut to my ear So I don't have to hear him say – he's turned away. Obsession! A tempest whirling around and round. This passion, a vision lost and so nearly found. Obsession! But does he share it at all? Flaring gold as the sunflowers that I painted – to hang on Gauguin's wall.

[OBSESSION]

"SUNFLOWERS"
Arles, 1888
van Gogh Museum, Amsterdam

29

LA BERCEUSE [MOTHER O MOTHER]

Vincent sees in the postman's wife Mme. Roulin, his ideal of the universal mother. He absorbs her face and visualizes sailors far far away in distant ports, whose only comfort is memories of a distant loving mother. He paints her five different times, always serenely rocking the cradle, always wearing the look of peaceful acceptance and stoic forbearance. In the spirit of his affection for her, arose La Berceuse, a lullaby to a mother from a lonesome and longing child. It is a paean to every mother who ever loved her child and longed for its happiness.

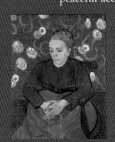

Out of the cradle endlessly rocking, adrift on the ocean of time. I'm comforted by a sweet lullaby that soothes me with color and rhyme. When I am bent so low I am breaking, your image appears in my eyes. Remembered embrace, imagined sweet face. I'm hopeful but not always wise. Mother O Mother, I feel you beside me. Hold me and gentle me, watch me and guide me. Mother O Mother, who ever loved me, or knew me as true as you? I am a sailor seeking safe harbor; fighting my storms of regret. I'm tossed with a force on waves of remorse, so far from the course that I've set. Never forsake me, never forget me, for I am the child of your heart. Like wind blows a flame, just whisper my name. I'll hear you though we'll be apart. Mother O Mother, I feel you beside me. Hold me and gentle me, watch me and guide me. Mother O Mother, who ever loved me, or knew me as true as you? Mother O Mother – I'll keep on singing La Berceuse to you.

"LA BERCEUSE" (Portrait of Madame Roulin)
Arles, 1889
Kröller-Müller Museum, Otterlo

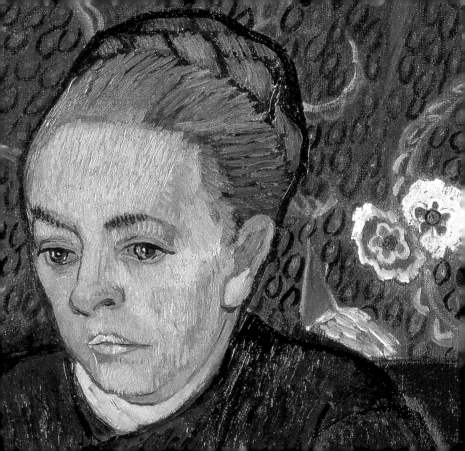

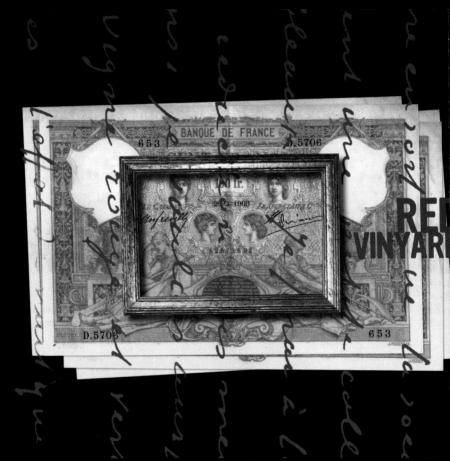

We have envisioned this song not in Arles, where it was painted, but in the asylum in St. Rémy, Vincent's home when this, the only painting he sold during his lifetime, was bought for 400 French francs by the painter Anna Boch. It is at once joy and disgust that he feels as he faces his piteous lack of recognition by the art world. Gauguin is the toast of Paris, yet Vincent is hidden away in an asylum, seemingly remembered only by his devoted brother Theo. We have conjured a lost letter from the tormented Vincent to Theo, in which passionate anger and childlike delight mingle and clash on his being told of his first sale.

"RED VINYARD"
Arles, 1888
Pushkin Museum, Moscow

LOST LETTER TO THEO]

One lousy stinking painting. After all these years of waiting, Theo. And she'll still have the painting when the money's spent and long gone, Theo, Theo...400 francs – what my efforts are worth for a painting of the earth. Poppies are growing up over my head. Long live the painter, long after he's dead. They'll wait till I'm moldering in my grave. The soul that no-one but you could ever save. I really sold a painting, after all these years of waiting, Theo. She really loves my painting of the workers toiling in the vineyard, Theo... 400 francs – quite a sum that we got for a painter time forgot. Poppies are growing up over my head. Long live the painter, long after he's dead. The fool with the easel who tried to compete. But oh – to prove them wrong – would be sweet. From my scathing reviews I can see, they can paint my work better than me. Curse the bastards who'd stand in my way! Oh, Theo...Hang my work on a hook on the wall. Not some dank musty cold empty hall. In Auvers, maybe in a café. Oh,

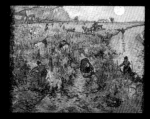

Theo...Oh, Theo...Oh, Theo! So you're a father now, Theo. I've gotta break this connection. You have better things to do – than worry about me. I hear Gauguin is doing well – they love him in Paris. It's just so hard to watch...

We imagine Vincent standing at the edge of a wide wheatfield illuminated by a sliver of moon, the stars blotted by inky clouds, the wide wings of crows circling overhead. He hallucinates that the wheat is rushing toward him, the sky pressing down. Shattered by the madness that closes in, he clings to the slim thread that connects him to his sanity, a longing for the freedom of the crows to simply fly away.

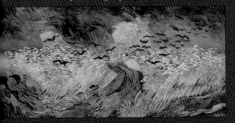

WHEATFIELD WIT
[EDGE OF THE WORL

34

I wish I could fly like a black crow. I'd spread my wings and I'd just go. Across the bridges I have burned. Back to my innocence returned. I wish I could fly like a black crow. And through the raging winds I'd go, above the waving wheat below. But here I am – only a man…Standing on the edge of the world. Feeling the rush. Feeling the crush of the madness. But I can see beyond the sadness – Standing on the edge of the world. Will this be an end – or a crossroads? No turning back to the lost roads. The

darkling sky draws in on me. The wheatfield is an angry sea. Will this be an end – or a crossroads? And I am poised to fly away. Jump on a crow's back – I can't stay. My soul's rebirth out of this earth. Standing on the edge of the world. Feeling the rush, feeling the crush of the madness. But I can see beyond the sadness. Standing on the edge of the world…Or will the picture fade to black…In this fast-moving, slow-aching, life-giving, heart-breaking, wonderful and terrible world.

"WHEATFIELDS WITH CROV
Auvers-sur-Oise, 18
van Gogh Museum, Amsterd

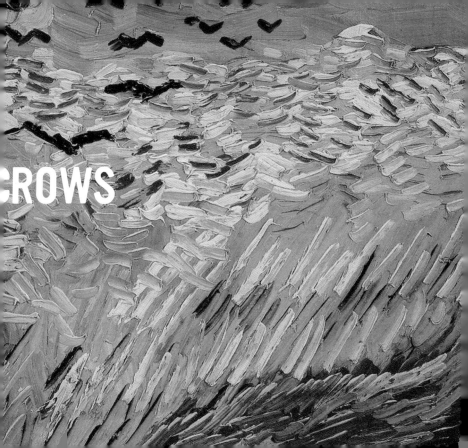

CROWS

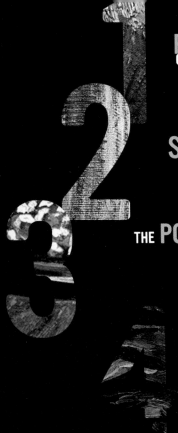

PORTRAIT OF THE ARTIST [PICTURE OF A MAN] 4:40

Reggie Hamilton – Bass
James Harrah – Guitar
Larry Aberman – Drums
Alan Steinberger – Pianos
Tom Harriman – Accordion, percussion & background vocals

SIEN WITH CIGAR SITTING ON THE [STILL LIFE] 4:42 FLOOR NEAR STOVE

Reggie Hamilton – Bass
James Harrah – Guitars
Larry Aberman – Drums
Tom Harriman – Keys, programming, background vocal

THE POTATO EATERS [ONE OF THE FAMILY] 3:48

Reggie Hamilton – Bass
James Harrah – Guitar
Peter Erskine – Drums
Alan Steinberger – Piano, B-3
Tom Harriman – additional keyboards, percussion

A PAIR OF SHOES [ONE FOOT IN FRONT OF THE OTHER] 3:47

Reggie Hamilton – Bass
James Harrah – Acoustic guitar
Larry Aberman – Drums
Alan Steinberger – Piano solo
Tom Harriman – Keyboards, programming

THE **BRIDGE** IN THE **RAIN**
[SHOW ME WHAT'S OVER THE BRIDGE] 4:24

Reggie Hamilton – Bass
James Harrah – Electric guitar
Marty Friedman – Guitar solo
Larry Aberman – Drums
Tom Kurai, Gary St. Germain of the Taiko Center of Los Angeles – Taiko
Tom Harriman – Keyboards, programming.
Background vocals arranged and performed by
Ken Stacy, Windy Wagner & Tom Harriman

FISHING BOATS ON THE BEACH AT **LES SAINTES-MARIES-DE-LA-MER**
[RED BOATS, GREEN] 5:45

Keyboards and programming – Tom Harriman

TERRACE OF A **CAFÉ** AT **NIGHT** [LA BELLE DE NUIT] 4:11

Alan Steinberger – Keyboards
James Harrah – Guitar
Tom Harriman – Keyboards, programming, background vocals

THE **YELLOW** HOUSE
[SEASON OF DREAMS] 3:55

Reggie Hamilton – Bass
James Harrah – Guitars
Larry Aberman – Drums
Tom Harriman – Piano, accordion, percussion, background vocals

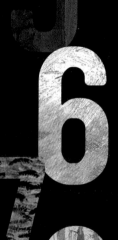

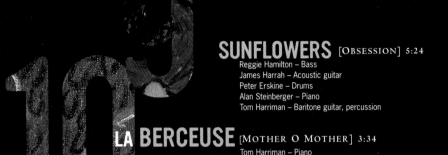

SUNFLOWERS [Obsession] 5:24

Reggie Hamilton – Bass
James Harrah – Acoustic guitar
Peter Erskine – Drums
Alan Steinberger – Piano
Tom Harriman – Baritone guitar, percussion

LA BERCEUSE [Mother O Mother] 3:34

Tom Harriman – Piano
James Harrah – Acoustic guitar
Andrew Shulman – Cello solo

RED VINYARD [Lost Letter to Theo] 4:43

Reggie Hamilton – Bass
James Harrah – Guitar
Marty Friedman – Guitar solo
Larry Aberman – Drums
Tom Harriman – Keyboards, programming, background vocals

WHEATFIELDS WITH CROWS [Standing On the Edge] 4:11

Reggie Hamilton – Bass
James Harrah – Guitar
Alan Steinberger – Piano
Tom Harriman – Drums, keyboards, programming

Strings on tracks 2, 9, 10 and 11
Violins: Tereza Stanislav (Concert Master),
Darius Campo, Larry Greenfield, Gerry Hilera,
Nancy Roth, Frank Tang, Miwako Watanabe,
John Wittenberg, Margaret Wooten, Ken Yerke
Celli: Andrew Shulman (Principal),
Mary Ann Lakatos, Stefanie Fife
String Contractor: Suzie Katayama
Conductor: Tom Harriman
String Orchestrations: Tom Harriman, Alan Steinberger

Produced and Arranged by Tom Harriman
(except tracks 1, 4, 7 & 12 produced with Allen Isaacs)

Associate producer: Pamela Phillips Oland
Executive Producer, Karla Hoff for Private Sound Records

Mixed by: Allen Isaacs
(except track 11 mixed by Tom Harriman)
Recorded by: Allen Isaacs, Charlie Paakkari & Tom Harriman

Additional engineers: Bradley Serna,
Brian Daugherty and Bill Smith

Mastered by: Dave Collins, Los Angeles, CA

Recorded at Capitol Studios, Hollywood, CA, USA
Additional recording at: Total Access Studios,
Redondo Beach, CA & Harriman Music, Studio City, CA

Art Direction and Design: Andy Engel
Design Production: Glenn Barry
Photography: Donald Miller
Liner Notes / Album Copy: Pamela Phillips Oland

Back-cover, pgs. 2–3 and 40, detail from "Self-Portrait
with Grey Felt Hat", Paris 1888, van Gogh Museum,
Amsterdam. Pg. 4, detail from "Wheatfields with
Crows", Auvers-sur-Oise, 1890, van Gogh Museum,
Amsterdam. Pg. 10, detail from "Self-Portrait", Arles,
1888, van Gogh Museum, Amsterdam. Pgs. 42–43,
"Vincent's Bedroom In Arles", Arles, 1888, van Gogh
Museum, Amsterdam.

Grammy® is the registered trademark of The National
Academy of Recording Arts & Sciences, Inc.

Special thanks
Deepest thanks to: my wife Karla, daughter Gwendolyn, and
Stefanie, Claudia & Alexander, for your love and unwavering
belief in me; My Father - my biggest fan – from a cloud of your
pipe smoke; Alex Mulder, for your friendship and tremendous
encouragement; The entire management and staff of the
van Gogh Museum, Amsterdam, for providing your extraordinary
support and resources. To Dominique Janssens of the Maison de
Van Gogh at Auvers-sur-Oise – for your steadfast dedication to
the cause Van Gogh; Pamela Phillips Oland & Tom Harriman
for your close friendship and professionalism; to Pamela for
imagining Vincent's lyrical point of view; and special thanks to
Tom for your extraordinary arrangements and brilliant world-class
productions; Andy Engel for your divinely-inspired artistry in
developing this packaging; Allen Isaacs for your dedication to
this project; Alan, James, Reggie, and Larry, musicians who go
that extra mile; Marty Friedman – Vincent would've loved your
passion; John Acosta of Musicians Local 47 for all your help;
The late Freddy Heineken for your esteemed friendship, and
PLAXO for the remarkable confluence of events which brought
me to Pamela & Tom; QüA Design team for your innovations;
Don Miller for photos; John Vis – shrink, pal, and foremost
l'homme du train; The uplifting and inspiring Montecatini Boys;
Erik Hazelhoff Roelfzema, a glass that's never "half empty;"
Miquel Ybanez, a shoulder I can always lean on; Tom van der Meer
for your twin gifts of friendship and wisdom; Bradley Serna –
smile on; Paula Salvatore, Capitol Studios, Wyn Davis, Total
Access Studios, and John Sabel for all your help.

And most of all…To VINCENT VAN GOGH, for your extraordinary
genius, vision, and singularly stunning artwork, which has thrilled,
inspired, and deeply moved generations of art lovers worldwide.
This album is a tribute to you, honoring the joy your formidable
talent has contributed to mankind.

From my heart, I thank you all – Diederick van Eck.

PRIVATE SOUND

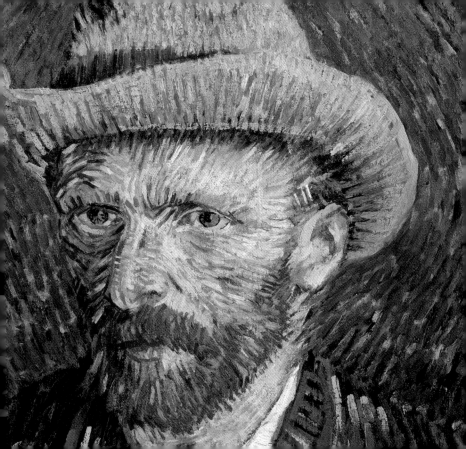

"How rich art is...
 one is never without food for thought or truly lonely."

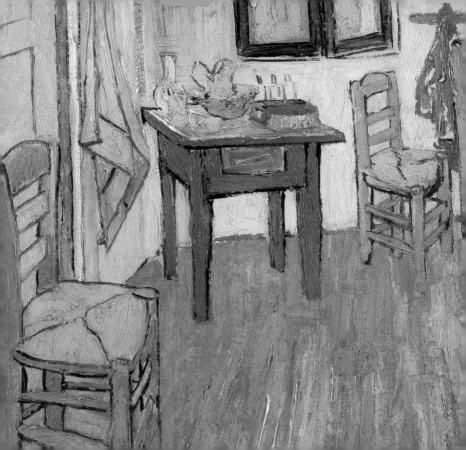

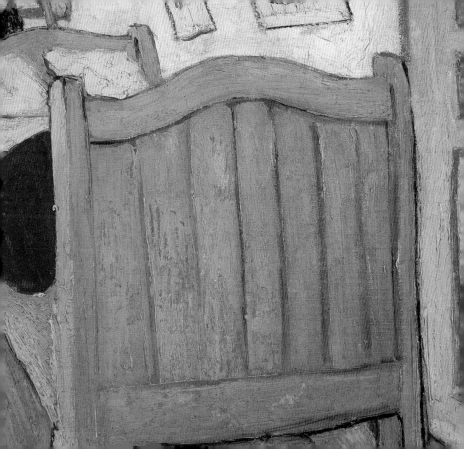